AF604700

For the students of Kongwak Primary School, who were inspired by Mr Beaky to learn about connection, identity and country. C.L.

For Sully. S.L.

First published in 2022 by

wild dog

PO Box 135
Fitzroy VIC 3065
Australia
wdog.com.au

Printed and bound in China by Everbest Printing Investment Limited

ISBN: 9781742036533

A catalogue record for this book is available from the National Library of Australia

10 9 8 7 6 5 4 3 2 1   22 23 24 25

FSC® is a non-profit international organisation established to promote the responsible management of the world's forests.

An **important message** from Mr Beaky

CASSIE LEATHAM & SUE LAWSON

wild dog

“Wumindjeka Daungwurrung Biik.”

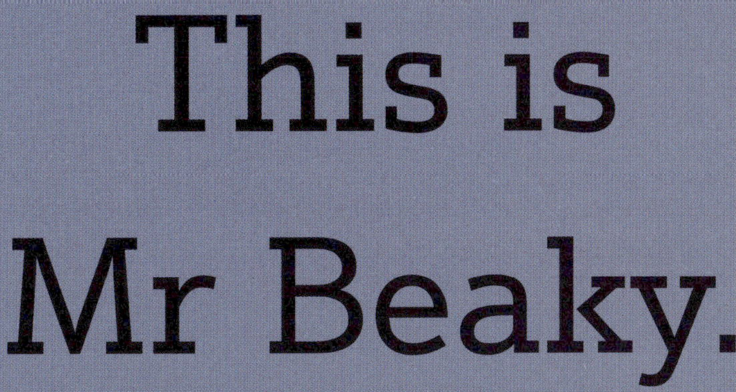

This is
Mr Beaky.

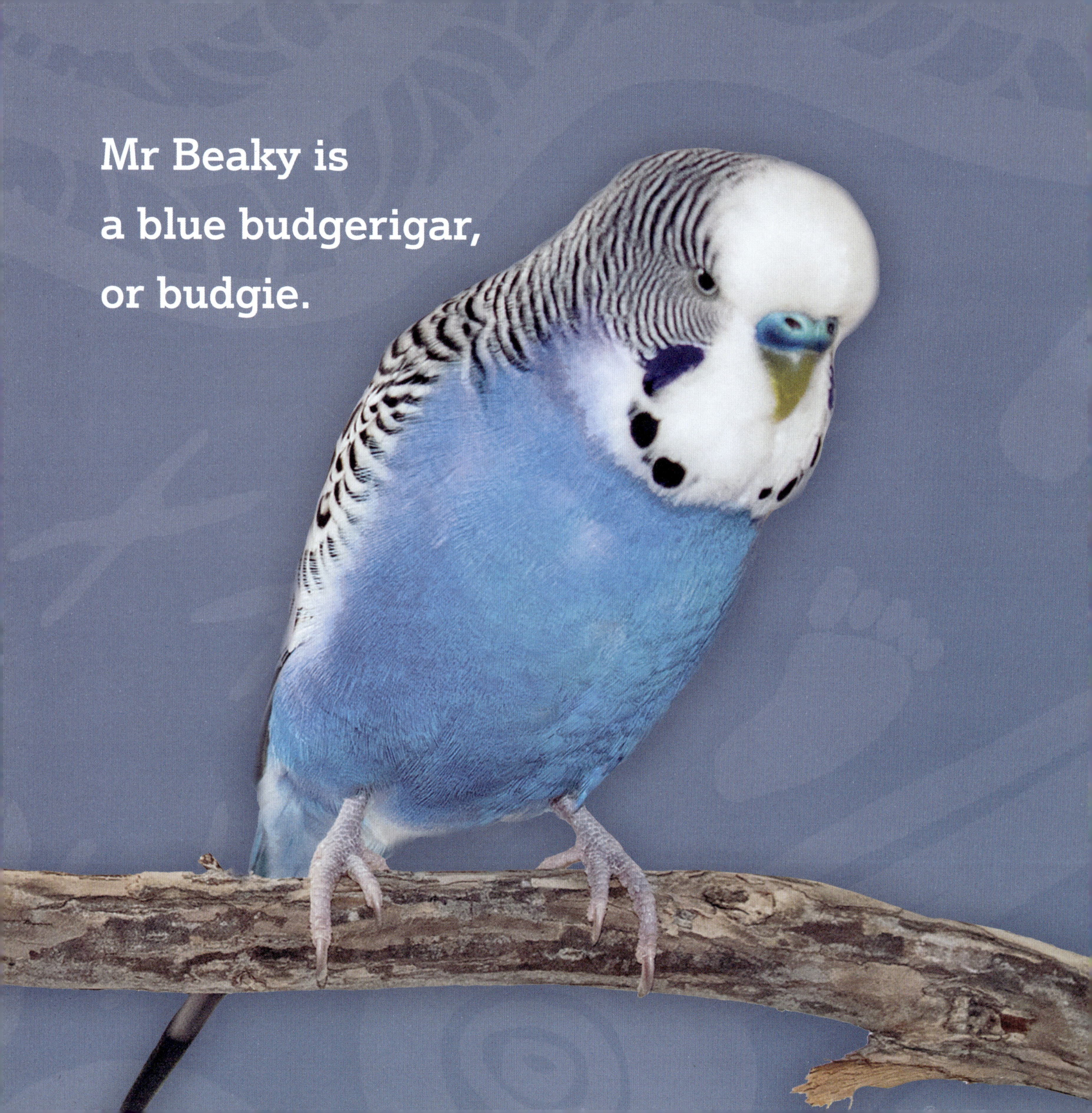

Mr Beaky is
a blue budgerigar,
or budgie.

He lives on Taungurung Country, which is part of the Kulin Nation in Victoria.

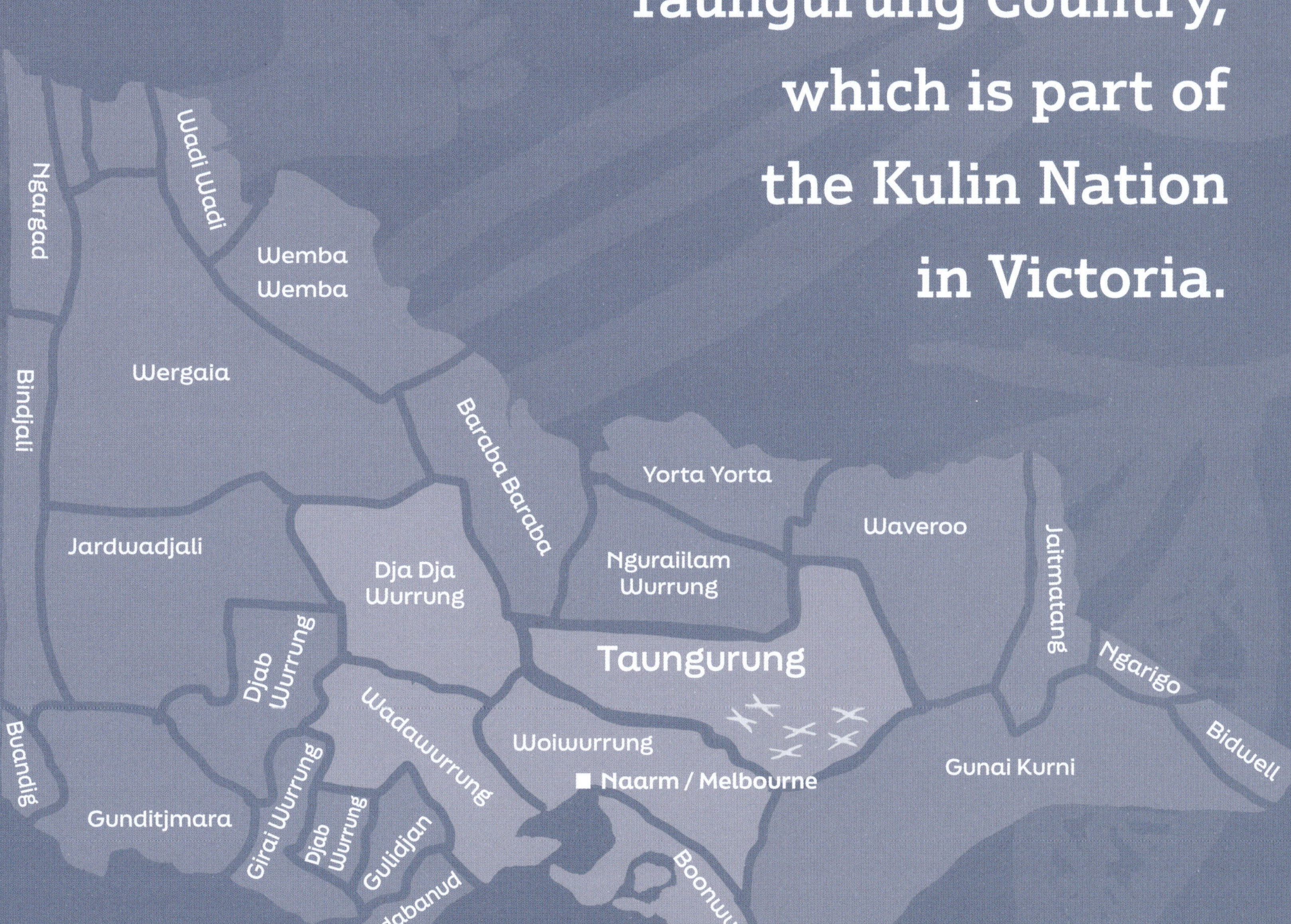

Mr Beaky can speak different languages.

The word

"budgerigar"

comes from the

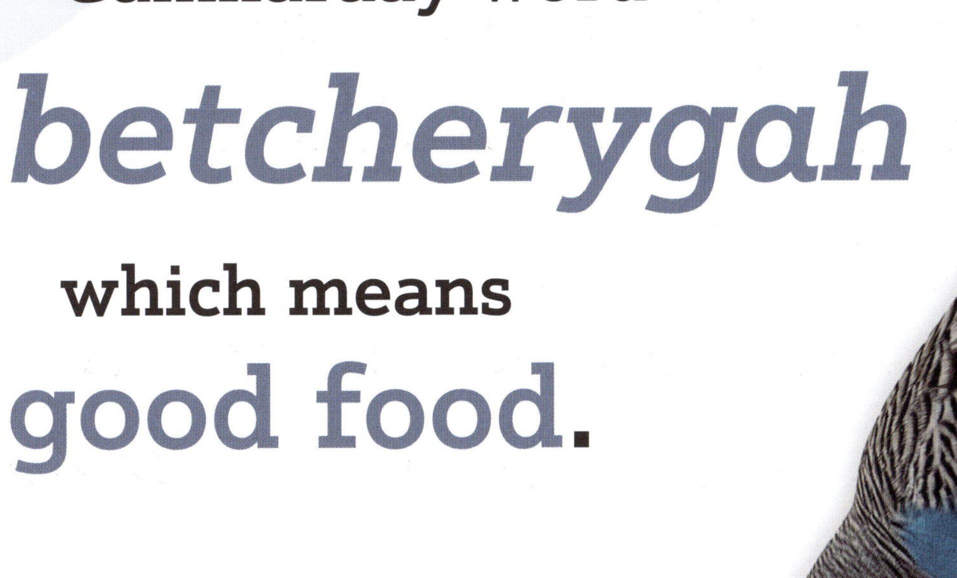

Gamilaraay word

betcherygah

which means

good food.

A budgerigar is a small parakeet, native to Australia.

In the wild, budgies have yellow and green feathers.

They have black markings on their cheeks and wings.

Pet budgies can have many shades of yellow, green, blue or white feathers.

"Just because *I'm* not green doesn't mean I can't be seen."

You are *blue*, not green and yellow.

But I am **still** a budgie!

“Always will be a blue budgie called Mr Beaky.”

Mr Beaky wants you to know that colour doesn’t decide who you are or where you fit.

Who you are is in your **murrup**.

Mr Beaky says, like him,
Aboriginal people
can look different too.

Aboriginal people can
have dark or light skin.
Black or red or brown
or yellow hair.
Brown or blue or
green eyes.

Being Aboriginal
is in your murrup.

"Always was, always will be Aboriginal Land."

Mr Beaky knows Aboriginal people are Australia's traditional owners – part of the world's longest continuing civilisation.

Aboriginal people have lived on, and cared for Country for more than **60,000 years**.

That's a *long*, ***long*** time.

Aboriginal culture is older than the pyramids, and they are ***old***.

Aboriginal people on Country

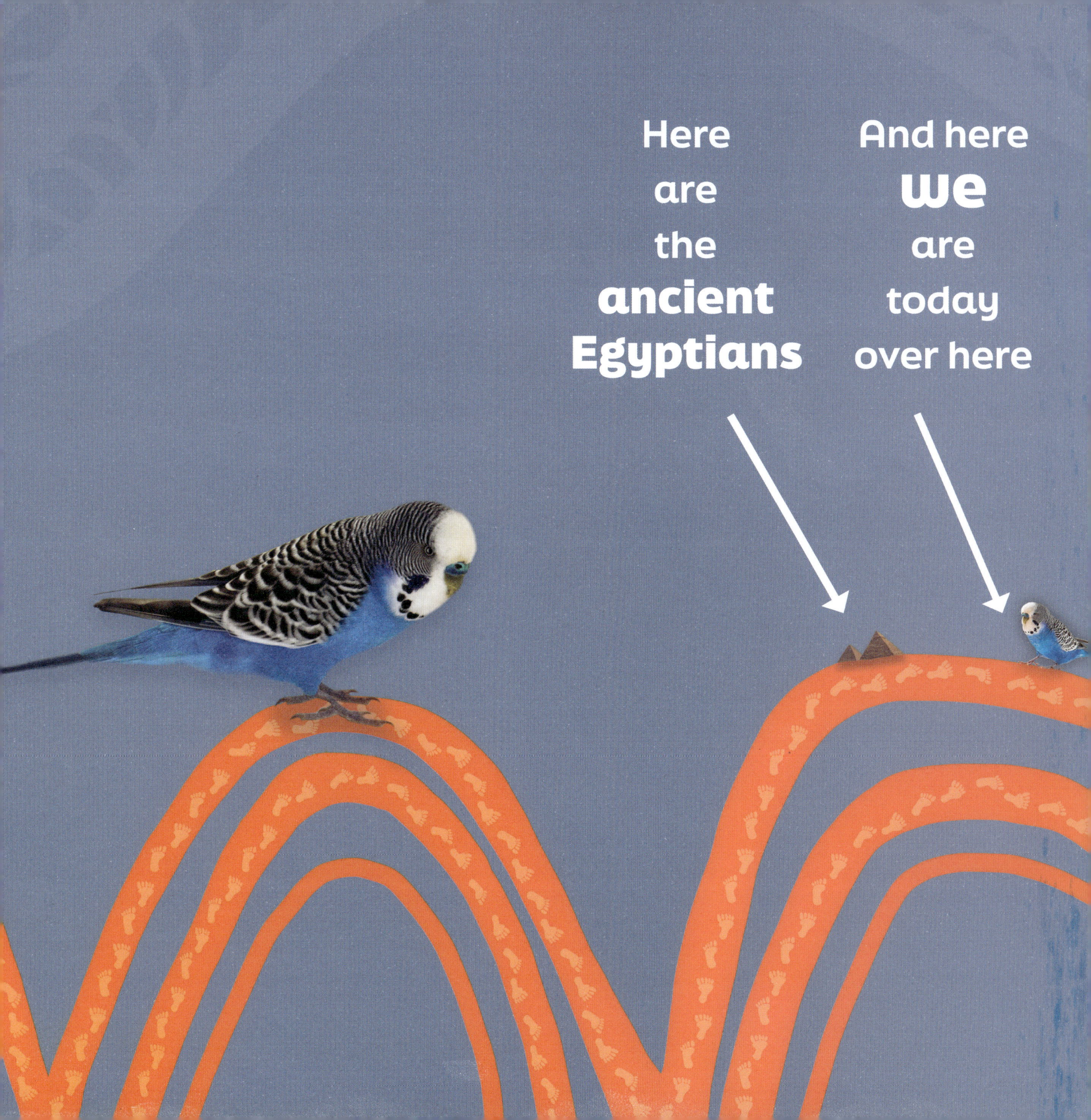
Here are the **ancient Egyptians**
And here **we** are today over here

“Dadbagi-k Biik.”

Mr Beaky says we must
care for Country.
Country is land and water.
It is animals and fish.
Trees and grass.
Elders and Ancestors.
You and me.

We're
all
connected.

**“Gilbruk Liwik.
Gilbruk Biik.”**

Mr Beaky says to care for Country,
we must listen to and respect
our Elders,
our Country,
so we, and Country,
can be healthy.

“Ngun Godjin.”

Mr Beaky says
thank you
for listening to his
important message,
thank you
for caring for Country.

Ngun
Godjin

Budgie Business

- Budgerigars are small birds, about 18–20 cm from head to tail. Each budgie can have up to 3000 feathers.

- Budgerigars mate for life. They nest in tree trunks, branches and even timber fence posts. The female lays up to eight eggs. The chicks hatch after 18 days and leave the nest after about 35 days.

- In the wild, budgerigars are found in Australia's interior. They migrate north, in search of rainfall and seeding grass. They eat seeds, grains and nuts from native herbs and grasses. After rain, there can be thousands of budgerigars in one flock.

- Budgerigars are important to Aboriginal people. Aboriginal clans watched for budgerigar flocks and followed them to water.

- Wild budgerigars are green and yellow – pet budgies can be many colours, including green, blue, aqua, turquoise, lilac, yellow, grey or white.

Glossary

parakeet: small to medium-sized parrot native to Australia

Biik: Country

dadbagi-k Biik: care for Country

Daungwurrung: Taungurung

murrup: soul and spirit – more than heart

gilbruk: respect

Liwik: Elders

ngun godjin: thank you

wumindjeka biik: hello, welcome

About Mr Beaky

Mr Beaky shares special stories of caring for Country and his walkabout journeys with children. Mr Beaky lives in Gippsland with his mob – Cassie, Kevin and Ryley.

About Cassie

Cassie Leatham is from the Taungurung people from the Kulin Nation. She is an artist, master weaver, traditional dancer, bushtukka woman and educator. Cassie is passionate about giving people opportunities to learn and understand Aboriginal culture.